Hope in the hearing

A 30 DAY DEVOTIONAL EMPOWERING
YOU TO HEAR GOD IN YOUR EVERYDAY LIFE

WENDY HENLEY

Elani
PUBLISHING

Hope in the Hearing
Copyright 2019 by Wendy Henley

All Scripture quotations, unless otherwise indicated, are taken from The Passion Translation (TPT) The Passion Translation. Copyright 2017 by BroadStreet Publishing Group, LLC. Used by permission. All rights reserved. thePassionTranslation.com. Scriptures marked AMP are taken from the AMPLIFIED BIBLE (AMP): Scripture taken from the AMPLIFIED BIBLE, Copyright 1954, 1958, 1962, 1964, 1965, 1987 by the Lockman Foundation Used by Permission. Scriptures marked NKJV are taken from the NEW KING JAMES VERSION (NKJV): Scripture taken from the NEW KING JAMES VERSION. Copyright 1982 by
Thomas Nelson, Inc. Used by permission. All rights reserved. Scripture taken from The Message. Copyright 1993, 1994, 1995, 1996, 2000, 2001, 2002. Used by permission of NavPress Publishing Group

For information contact :
http://www.elanipublishing.com

Cover design & Interior Layout by Peter Mitchell
Cover Photography by Andrea Calvary

ISBN: 978-0-578-52883-0

First Edition: July 2019

Endorsements

"I love teaching people simple effective tools to learn to hear the voice of God for themselves. That is exactly what Wendy has created here with this devotional. The Holy Spirit speaks to us in so many multifaceted ways. Wendy created a jewel here that not only helps the new believer but also inspires the seasoned believer to explore those different facets and steward the message. Prepare to be empowered and inspired to go deeper in your journey getting to know the person of God in your everyday lives as you use this tool for a launch pad. It is so much fun learning to dialogue with God. "

Sid Widmer – Prophetic Trainer

"Wendy's approach to recognizing the voice of God is so refreshing! I love how Wendy brings the reader into a delightful journey in recognizing the voice of God in a way that is so practical. She's make it so easy and attainable! This will become a resource to all who desire to hear the Lord in their everyday life. Read this and be prepared to be engaged, inspired and encouraged!"

Deseree Gonzales – Kingdom Culture Ministries

"I CAN hear God's voice!" For many years I thought it was impossible to really hear God speak, so my relationship with Him involved frustration, and a belief that there was something wrong with me for not being able to enjoy a more intimate relationship with the Father. But through this simple process Wendy shares, I'm filled with hope and anticipation in my spirit! I do see God, I do hear Him speak, and He does show His love, wisdom, and His ways to me. Thank you, Wendy, for this simple yet effective process to hear the voice of God and to know the heart of God; because to know God, is to love God.

"If you look for me, you will find me, if you look for me with all your heart."

Pastor Becky Hennesy – Trinity Church Cedar Hill

"It is one thing when an author writes from a place of theory and information but it is another thing when an author writes from a place of revelation and breakthrough! When an author writes from a place of breakthrough revelation it has the ability to become a weapon of transformation within the hands of the reader. Wendy Henley has done just that! This devotional is an infusion of revelation and practical wisdom that will ignite and activate the voice of God within you! Get ready to receive an upgrade in your ability to recognize the voice of God!"

Matt Gonzales – Kingdom Culture Ministries

Dedication

This book is dedicated to my incredible family- TJ, Caleb, and Zoe, you have loved me fiercely and cheered me on to be the woman I am! I love you with all of my heart!

Acknowledgments

I want to acknowledge the amazing people God has put in my life that helped make this book happen! Thank you to all my parents: Dan and Glenda, I love you! Ted and Donna, thank you for loving me as your daughter. To my many, many sisters in Christ, especially my sis in love Jenny Henley, thank you!

Lovelies and Gathering Girls, you are my heart. Lonnie, Annette, and War Cry Ladies, thank you for letting me practice! To my incredible Pastor's Jim and Becky, you have built a platform under me and covered me with love-

To Tony Strain for prophesying over me 24 years ago that I would teach the things of the Spirit. For my amazing School of the Prophets forever family: Sid, Daneen, Becki, David Michael, and Kenneth you all are irreplaceable!

To Matt and Desi for sharing your heart, lives, and word of the Lord, so thankful

Andrea Calvary, your photo carries His essence and imprint- so grateful

Valerie and Anika at Elani Publishing, you made it happen!

To All of the many people who are not personally named here that have prayed for me, supported me with love, encouraged me, and been so faithful.

Forever Grateful- Wendy

Introduction

I have always desired to hear God, to know He cared about my everyday life. The first time I read Psalm 139, I was encouraged to believe that this was in fact the case! So, if He is everywhere, knowing my every move, then couldn't He be speaking to me all the time as well? Could it be that I was just not aware of His precious whispers?

This thought warmed my, and my eyes sparkle...God could be speaking to me all the time! This also raised more questions: So how would I know? Did I have to hear Him in an audible voice? Answering these and other questions began my journey of finding out how God can speak to us in our everyday lives. I was determined to know how He was communicating His precious love, giving me direction, and how answering these questions could help others on their journeys.

I love nature and have an affinity for all things outdoors. Whether I was gardening, hiking, skiing, or just going for a walk, I found myself praying.

For me it's been two fold. I also like to be moving, so once I combined movement with Creation, it felt very natural to connect with Creator God.

It was in these times that I found myself pouring out my heart and feeling so heard by the Lord; and then things would happen after I asked Him to reveal Himself to me,

counsel me, or just love on my heart.

I began to notice birds, insects, and even plants; it was as though they were bringing me sweet messages from the Father. Right when I was feeling alone, and longing for His presence to be near, I would see a lovely dove close by. When I would cry out for Him to fill me with His joy, a butterfly would show up, flittering all around me as I ran. I once even had a turtle show up in my backyard right by the patio where I had my quiet times, reminding me that slow can also be steady in the race of life.

You see, God is faithful. He loves to speak to His children in ways they CAN hear and know it's Him. While He is magnificent and far beyond what we could think or imagine, He is relational at His core.

This was crucial for me to understand before I could count on the fact that He actually wanted to speak to me, and not to just obey

instructions. I had to un-think some things I had thought about His character. This required prayer, time in His word, and listening to mature believers who had experienced the goodness His word refers to.

Here are some key verses that anchor my heart and encourage me of His goodness as well as His desire to speak to me.

John 10:4-5

"And when he brings out his own sheep, he goes before them; and the sheep follow him, for they know his voice. 5 Yet they will by no means follow a stranger, but will flee from him, for they do not know the voice of stranger."

Galatians 5:22-25

"22 But the fruit of the Spirit is love, joy, peace, longsuffering, kindness, goodness, faithfulness, 23 [g]gentleness, and self-control. Against such there is no law. 24 And those who are Christ's have crucified the flesh with its passions and desires. 25 If we live in the Spirit, let us also walk in the Spirit. 26 Let us not become conceited, provoking one another, envying one another."

The goal of this devotion is to not only cultivate your relationship with His word, but to activate you in hearing His voice in your everyday life. I have found that the more we honor and are aware of Him communicating with us, the more we will be awakened to His presence all around us!

The Plan

Each day will encompass a short lesson with scripture and an activation. This devotional is interactive and is designed to awaken and develop hope in every believer so that you can hear the Lord not only for yourselves, but for others! The format will include:

1) Stating three things you are grateful for/ gratitude statements

2) Starting on Day 2, you will be stating how the Lord spoke to you the day before (this is an honoring by being grateful for Him pursuing us in various ways)

3) Scripture and short lesson

4) Activation and journal- this is where you apply what you are reading, and build momentum to hear more!

Now, let's dive into this journey of hearing His voice, seeing His hand move, watching Him reveal His beauty around us, and walking in the freedom of knowing His heart for our lives!

DAY 1

Good Day To You!

Let's start with 3 things you are grateful for today:

_____

_____

_____

_____

Scripture

Romans 5:5

"And this hope is not a disappointing fantasy, because we can now experience the endless love of God cascading into our hearts the Holy Spirit who lives in us!"

This scripture is so powerful to me! When I read scripture, I look for words that just POP out to me and I ask the Holy Spirit why those words pop. So looking at it from that perspective, what words are popping out to YOU right now?

_____

_____

_____

_____

Activation

Take a moment to think about some words that you keep hearing in conversations this past week or over the last month. There may be one word that you have heard over and over and have thought to yourself, "Wow, I've heard that same word 3x this week..."

Now ask the Lord what He is wanting to say to you with this word. Take time to just be still and listen. What pictures might be coming to your mind? Do other words associated to that word pop in your mind?
Write it all down!

_____

_____

_____

_____

_____

_____

_____

Notes

_____
_____
_____
_____
_____
_____
_____
_____
_____
_____
_____
_____
_____
_____
_____
_____
_____
_____
_____
_____
_____
_____

Notes

DAY 2

Hello Friend!

Let's start with 3 things you are grateful for today:

_____

_____

_____

_____

Honoring God Speaking

Now, reflecting on yesterday or this past week, what is one way you could sense, see, or hear Papa God speaking to you? (i.e. the same song kept playing that struck a chord in your heart; you heard a phrase or word several times in a matter of days, you saw a particular animal you identify with during prayer, or your child came up and asked a question out of nowhere that seemed straight from Heaven)

_____

_____

_____

_____

_____

_____

_____

Scripture

Romans 15:13 TPT

"Now may God, the inspiration and fountain of hope, fill you to overflowing with uncontainable joy and perfect peace as you trust in Him. And may the power of the Holy Spirit continually surround your life with His super-abundance until you radiate with hope!"

Highlight or underline the words that are leaping off the page to you, then write down the significance of those words to you.

There are so many precious things in this scripture verse. I love that His joy is uncontainable, that His peace is perfect and anchors us in every storm. I love that He is trustworthy in every circumstance and that He does not just give a little, but He gives a super-abundance of hope that causes us to literally light up!

_____

_____

_____

_____

Activation

What is an area of your life that you need super-abundant joy in?

_____

_____

_____

_____

_____

_____

Now Ask Papa God to fill you with that joy ... Today claim this scripture over that area as many times as you think of it; thank Papa God for all He is doing in it and all He is going to do!

Notes

_____

_____

_____

_____

_____

_____

_____

_____

_____

_____

_____

_____

_____

_____

_____

_____

_____

_____

_____

_____

_____

_____

Notes

DAY 3

Hello Joyful One!

What three things are you grateful for today?

_____

_____

_____

_____

Honoring God Speaking

Now, reflecting on yesterday, what is one way you could sense, see, or hear Papa God speaking to you? (i.e. the same song kept playing in your mind; a certain animal or insect kept making its way into your view, a friend texted you just the right words)

_____

_____

_____

_____

_____

_____

Scripture

Hebrews 11:1 AMP

"Now faith is the assurance (title deed, confirmation) of things hoped for (divinely guaranteed), and the evidence of things not seen [the conviction of their reality—faith comprehends as fact what cannot be experienced by the physical senses.]

Wow...What leapt off the page to you?

_____

_____

_____

_____

Hope is the seed of faith. If we lose our hope, we cannot have faith for what we long to see happen in this world. Sometimes, it's just a matter of asking Him to restore our hope in a situation so that we can pray in faith about it. I often ask the Lord to show me the situation or person through His eyes to help shift my perspective. This simple act opens my heart to hope again for that situation or person.

Activation

Ask Holy Spirit what situation or person you are feeling hopeless about.

Now ask Him to restore your hope and let you see it through His lens. Begin to thank Him for restoring your hope to have faith that all things will work for good in this! Then ask Him for a hug today to encourage your heart in this area. Listen for His voice in a song He brings, the words of a friend, scripture, or even something in nature that only He would know you enjoy.

Notes

_____

_____

_____

_____

_____

_____

_____

_____

_____

_____

_____

_____

_____

_____

_____

_____

_____

_____

_____

_____

_____

_____

_____

_____

_____

_____

_____

_____

_____

_____

_____

_____

_____

_____

_____

_____

_____

_____

_____

_____

_____

_____

_____

DAY 4

Hello Mighty One!

What three things are you grateful for today?

_____

_____

_____

_____

Honoring God Speaking

Now, reflecting on yesterday, what is one way you could sense, see, or hear Papa God speaking to you?

_____

_____

_____

_____

_____

_____

_____

Romans 8:28 TPT

"So we are convinced that every detail of our lives is continually woven together to fit into God's perfect plan of bringing good into our lives, for we are His lovers who have been called to fulfill his designed purpose."

What is landing in your heart from this scripture?

_____

_____

_____

_____

I love how in the Passion Translation it says "every detail woven together to fit into God's perfect plan..."
I love that in the mystery of God, He is still so personal. He has such a brilliance about His being that allows Him to orchestrate macro and micro-cosmism.
He sets the stars in place, yet still knows the hairs on my head...He cares about the details and His presence orchestrates my life!

Activation

What details have you noticed God has paid attention to that warmed your heart and made you smile? (Example: I was really missing my Son away at college and he showed up at church out of the blue! Another example is that I really wanted to go back to California one year and an event that God provided for popped up; it was more than I imagined!)

_____

_____

_____

Now, think of something that you would like to see come to fruition that would make your heart smile and write it down here.

_____

_____

Notes

Notes

_____

_____

_____

_____

_____

_____

_____

_____

_____

_____

_____

_____

_____

_____

_____

_____

_____

_____

_____

_____

_____

DAY 5

Hello Hopeful One!

What three things are you grateful for today?

_____

_____

_____

_____

Honoring God Speaking

Now, reflecting on yesterday, what is one way you could sense, see, or hear Papa God speaking to you?

_____

_____

_____

_____

_____

_____

_____

_____

Scripture

Phil 4:7 TPT

"Tell Him every detail of your life, then God's wonderful peace that transcends human understanding, will make the answers known to you through Jesus Christ."

"Will make the answers known to you..." stood out to me because it shows He does not withhold information or His heart. He is gracious to reveal what He sees we need to know. He operates with such tender wisdom in revealing answers and solutions we need, not only for our lives, but for those around us as well. He is faithful beyond measure!

What tugged at your heart in this scripture?

_____

_____

_____

_____

Activation

Take your question to the Lord and ask Him to answer so specifically today. Be alert to Him answering in various ways. Document it when He does! Be prepared to share with a friend as well!

The more we honor God speaking to us, the more we are open to hear Him, see Him, sense Him, as well as know the language He uses to speak to us!

_____

_____

_____

_____

_____

_____

_____

Notes

_____

_____

_____

_____

_____

_____

_____

_____

_____

_____

_____

_____

_____

_____

_____

_____

_____

_____

_____

_____

_____

Notes

_____

_____

_____

_____

_____

_____

_____

_____

_____

_____

_____

_____

_____

_____

_____

_____

_____

_____

_____

_____

_____

_____

DAY 6

Hello Precious One!

What three things are you grateful for today?

_____

_____

_____

_____

Honoring God Speaking

Now, reflecting on yesterday, what is one way you could sense, see, or hear Papa God speaking to you?

_____

_____

_____

_____

_____

_____

_____

_____

Scripture

Isa. 40:29-31 TPT

"He gives power to the weak, And to those who have no might He increases strength. Even the youths shall faint and be weary, and the young men shall utterly fall, but those who wait on the Lord shall renew their strength; they shall mount up with wings like eagles, they shall run and not be weary, they shall walk and not faint."

How did this scripture speak to your heart?

_____

_____

_____

_____

This scripture encourages me because it shows His character of generosity and grace. He does not say God helps those who help themselves...He says He will give us POWER and increase strength when we are weak! We can come to Him in faith when we are feeling down, when we feel like we can't make it through, and know that when we ask, He has already said "YES" to help us! YES that's His will! YES to give us what we need, to not only make it, but to THRIVE because of His strength in us!!

Activation

Be still for 5 minutes today, outside if possible or close to a window with natural light...What are you hearing/ picking up?

_____

_____

_____

Notes

_____

_____

_____

_____

_____

_____

_____

_____

_____

_____

_____

_____

_____

_____

_____

_____

_____

_____

_____

_____

_____

Notes

_____

_____

_____

_____

_____

_____

_____

_____

_____

_____

_____

_____

_____

_____

_____

_____

_____

_____

_____

_____

_____

_____

DAY 7

Hello Glorious One!

What three things are you grateful for today?

_____

_____

_____

_____

Honoring God Speaking

Now, reflecting on yesterday, what is one way you could sense, see, or hear Papa God speaking to you?

_____

_____

_____

_____

_____

_____

_____

 *Scripture*

Psalms 65:5 TPT

"You answer our prayers with amazing wonders and with awe inspiring displays power. You are the righteous God that helps us like a Father. Everyone everywhere looks to you for are the confidence of all the earth, even to the farthest islands of the sea."

What stood out to you?

_____

_____

_____

_____

What stood out to me are the words "amazing wonders", "You are the confidence of the earth", and "inspiring displays of power."
The Lord truly wants to answer us beyond what we can think or imagine and I love how this scripture embodies the brilliance of that truth!

Activation

So since God is a God of wonders, let's try something new...what smells have you been picking up on lately? Good or bad? Now ask the Lord what He is saying through these smells. Is He revealing Beauty? Is He wanting to show you something about your circumstances? Your identity?

_____

_____

_____

_____

_____

Notes

Notes

DAY 8

Hello Warrior!

What three things are you grateful for today?

_____

_____

_____

_____

Honoring God Speaking

Now, reflecting on yesterday, what is one way you could sense, see, or hear Papa God speaking to you?

_____

_____

_____

_____

_____

_____

_____

Scripture

1 Peter 3:13-15 MSG

"'If with heart and soul you're doing good, do you think you can be stopped? Even if you suffer for it, you're still better off. Don't give the opposition a second thought. Through thick and thin, keep your hearts at attention, in adoration before Christ, your Master. Be ready to speak up and tell anyone who asks why you're living the way you are, and always with the utmost courtesy."

What pops out at you? Why?

_____

_____

_____

_____

What stood out to me was:

How it says that if your heart is good, who can stop you? WHO? Not even the enemy...which leads me to the next thing that was highlighted to me - Don't give the opposition a second thought...no time of the day...the enemy is powerless against Christ inside of you and if your mind and heart are set on Christ, the enemy does not deserve a second thought! And what is the best defense of that? Keeping our hearts at attention, and in complete adoration before Christ...Yes Lord!

Activation

I often see numbers, and relate them to scripture. For example: 5:13 am = I will ask Holy Spirit which book to look up Chapter 5 verse 13 in, in the Word. It hits home every time! He knows our heart and needs before we can articulate them!! What numbers have you been seeing lately?

_____

_____

_____

_____

_____

_____

_____

_____

_____

_____

_____

_____

_____

_____

_____

_____

_____

_____

_____

_____

_____

_____

_____

_____

_____

Notes

DAY 9

Hello Hopeful One!

What three things are you grateful for today?

_____

_____

_____

_____

Honoring God Speaking

Now, reflecting on yesterday, what way Papa did speak to you? Did you
sense anything in a way you have not before?

_____

_____

_____

_____

_____

_____

_____

Scripture

Proverbs 4:23 TPT

"So above all, guard the affections of your heart, for they affect all that you are. Pay attention to the welfare of your innermost being, for from there flows the wellspring of life."

What is Holy Spirit highlighting to you in this scripture?

_____

_____

_____

_____

This scripture reminds me that it's so easy in our daily lives to forget to guard our hearts from things that are not fruitful. Things like offense, bitterness, unforgiving, and fear. When we let those creep in, our springs are tainted, and cannot deliver the life giving waters to not only our own souls, but to those around us!

Activation

Ask the Holy Spirit to show you today through various means, any areas of your heart you have let go unguarded for a time. He may give you a scripture, a song, or a revelation as you are meditating on His goodness. Be open and aware today!

Notes

Notes

DAY 10

Hello Favored One!

What three things are you grateful for today?

_____

_____

_____

_____

Honoring God Speaking

Now, reflecting on yesterday, how did you hear Papa speak to you?
What did He say?

_____

_____

_____

_____

_____

_____

_____

_____

Scripture

Isaiah 43:1- 2 NKJV

"But now, thus says the Lord, who created you, O Jacob, and He who formed you, O Isreal: Fear not, for I have redeemed you; I have called you by your name; you are Mine. When you pass through the waters, I will be here with you; when you walk through the fire, you will not be burned, nor shall the flame scorch you."

What was highlighted to you in this scripture?

_____

_____

_____

_____

When I think about the Lord saying, "Fear Not" I get excited! It means that the Lord of the Universe has us covered! We could walk through rushing rivers, or fiery trials, and He is always with us. We don't have to worry about our performance, or making sure we are worthy because He has already redeemed us to do what He has called us to do! We not only have everything we need for today, but there is also nothing that can sweep us away!!

Activation

When you read "Fear Not..." what fear pops in your head? Ask the Holy Spirit what He wants you to do to face that fear. Do you need to confess it, change your mind about it? Do you need to ask someone to pray with you? Do you need to do all of these and meditate on scripture? Write down what you sense He is saying and make a plan to do that in the next couple of days, then journal how you feel afterwards.

_____

_____

_____

Notes

Notes

_____
_____
_____
_____
_____
_____
_____
_____
_____
_____
_____
_____
_____
_____
_____
_____
_____
_____
_____
_____
_____
_____

DAY 11

Hello Victorious One!

What three things are you grateful for today?

_____
_____
_____
_____

Honoring God Speaking

Now, reflecting on yesterday, how did you hear/ sense/ know Papa speaking to you?

_____
_____
_____
_____
_____
_____
_____
_____

Scripture

Colossians 1:21-22 TPT

"Even though you were once distant from him, living in the shadows of your evil thoughts and actions, He reconnected you back to Himself. He released His supernatural peace to you through the sacrifice of His own body as the sin-payment on your behalf so that you would dwell in His presence. And now there is nothing between you and the Father God, for He sees you as HOLY, FLAWLESS, and RESTORED..."

What made your spirit leap when you read this scripture?

_____

_____

_____

_____

Even when we were in the shadows, in shame, hiding, He sought us out, and reconnected us back to Himself. He released His supernatural peace to us...He sees us as connected; He sees us as set apart for Him; He sees us as flawless.... His love never fails, nor fails to reach us wherever we are, and wherever we have been.

Activation

Today pay attention when thoughts of unworthiness, shame, or feeling disconnected creep in. Thank the Lord for the above truth and then ask Him to tell you one of His favorite attributes about you.

Notes

_____

_____

_____

_____

_____

_____

_____

_____

_____

_____

_____

_____

_____

_____

_____

_____

_____

_____

_____

_____

_____

Notes

DAY 12

Good Day Amazing One!

What three things are you grateful for today?

_____

_____

_____

_____

Honoring God Speaking

Now, reflecting on yesterday, what way Papa did speak to you? Did you sense anything in a way you have not before?

_____

_____

_____

_____

_____

_____

_____

_____

Scripture

Hebrews 12:2

"We look away from the natural realm and we fasten our gaze onto Jesus who birthed faith within us and who leads us forward into faith's perfection. His example is this: Because his heart was focused on the joy of knowing that you would be his, he endured the agony of the cross and conquered its humiliation, and now sits exalted at the right hand of the throne of God!"

This scripture is rich! What is Holy Spirit highlighting to you?

_____

_____

_____

_____

When we focus on the Lord, our faith is perfected! We are not consumed by the things happening in the natural realm but rather how we can partner our faith with the faith Giver, the perfector, and change the atmosphere of the natural around us. We can bring His Kingdom to the earth!!

Activation

Spend just 5 minutes in worship communicating to the Lord how majestic He is and how He is faithful. Then sit and listen for 5 minutes. Journal what you see in your mind's eye, what you sense, or what you hear.

_____

_____

_____

Notes

_____

_____

_____

_____

_____

_____

_____

_____

_____

_____

_____

_____

_____

_____

_____

_____

_____

_____

_____

_____

_____

_____

_____

_____

_____

_____

_____

_____

_____

_____

_____

_____

_____

_____

_____

_____

_____

_____

_____

_____

_____

_____

_____

_____

DAY 13

Hello Faithful One!

What three things are you grateful for today?

_____

_____

_____

_____

Honoring God Speaking

Reflecting on yesterday, in what way Papa did speak to you and what did He say?

_____

_____

_____

_____

_____

_____

_____

_____

Psalms 13:6 TPT

"I will sing my song of joy to you, the Most High, for in all of this you have strengthened my soul...."
"I have thrown myself headlong into your arms—I'm celebrating your rescue. I'm singing at the top of my lungs, I'm so full of answered prayers." The Message

What did the Spirit highlight to you when you read these scriptures?

_____

_____

_____

_____

This scripture reminds me of the Song that says. "This is how I fight my battles..." We throw ourselves into His arms and we sing a song of joy! We sing over not only what He has already done. but what we know He is doing. and will do on our behalf! He does these things because He is GOOD. FAITHFUL. and KIND!

What ways can you identify with this? Is there a song. verse. or poem that comes to your mind when you consider the theme of this verse?

_____

_____

_____

_____

Activation

Sing spontaneously whatever comes to your heart for the next ten minutes. then journal any theme(s) that arise.

Notes

Notes

DAY 14

Hello Brilliant One!

What three things are you grateful for today?

_____

_____

_____

_____

Honoring God Speaking

Reflecting on yesterday. in what way Papa did speak to you?

_____

_____

_____

_____

_____

_____

_____

_____

Matt. 14:14-16

"And when Jesus went out He saw a great multitude; and He was moved with compassion for them, and healed their sick. When it was evening, the disciples came to Him, saying, "This is a deserted place, and the hour is already late. Send the multitudes away, that they may go into the villages and buy themselves food." But Jesus said to them, "They do not need to go away. You give them something to eat."

Wow... So what jumped out at you? Write down any words, or themes emphasized in your mind as you read.

_____

_____

_____

_____

As I ponder on this section of scripture, I notice how Jesus is moved with compassion for the people. First, He sees their need for healing, so He heals the sick. Then, rather than sending people away, He tells the disciples to be the solution!

He leads by example, doing the miraculous and healing their physical bodies. Then he calls the disciples up, to move on the compassion they are feeling by meeting needs of the crowd, miraculously. The only problem is, they don't fully understand how to do that. He is so gracious in His leadership that He, once again, sets the example for being the solution by multiplying the bread and fish. Jesus wants us to not just be moved by our compassion, but to know He has provided access to us to be solutions for those around us, not just with natural means, but also by multiplying supernatural means!

Activation

Ask the Holy Spirit to create in you a hunger and thirst for the things of the Kingdom. He is longing for us to partner with Him! Write down anything you hear as you are praying about this.

_____

_____

_____

_____

_____

_____

_____

_____

_____

_____

_____

_____

_____

_____

_____

_____

_____

_____

_____

_____

Notes

DAY 15

Hello Precious One!

What three things are you grateful for today?

_____

_____

_____

_____

Honoring God Speaking

Reflecting, in what ways has Papa been speaking to you this week?

_____

_____

_____

_____

_____

_____

_____

Scripture

Daniel 7:9-10 NKJV

"'I watched till thrones were put in place, and the Ancient of Days was seated; His garment was white as snow, and the hair of His head was like pure wool. His throne was a fiery flame, its wheels a burning fire; A fiery stream issued and came forth from before Him. A thousand thousands ministered to Him....'"

Draw a picture or describe in your own words what you saw in your mind's eye when you read this. What did it evoke in you?

_____

_____

_____

_____

The Lord is majestic! I am enamored with His beauty and holiness! I see the fire around His throne being a symbol of His burning passion and His utter consumption of anything that is not love based. He even opens the books to judge those things!

Activation

Meditate on the majesty of God. What pictures come to mind? What are you seeing, or do you see on a regular basis, when you think about His majesty?

_____

_____

_____

_____

_____

_____

Notes

_____

_____

_____

_____

_____

_____

_____

_____

_____

_____

_____

_____

_____

_____

_____

_____

_____

_____

Notes

DAY 16

Good Day Creative One!

What three things are you grateful for today?

_____

_____

_____

_____

Honoring God Speaking

Reflecting on yesterday, in what ways has Papa been speaking to you?

_____

_____

_____

_____

_____

_____

_____

Habakkuk 2:4

"Look at the proud one, his soul is not right with him, but the righteous will live by his faith [in the true God]."

Jot down what landed the most with you from this scripture:

_____

_____

_____

_____

The just shall live by faith- the word " live" in the Hebrew is "chayah" according to Strong's #2421. It means to be preserved and to flourish... our faith is in the Majestic one; our surety in His being brings life to us and causes us to flourish. It means we don't just live, we FLOURISH! Blessing you today with a depth of faith that causes you to live and flourish in the glory of His majesty!

Activation

Take 5 minutes to think about how faitful God has been to you. Write down as many ways as you can think of.

_____

_____

Now, write down this scripture or a different scripture, that will remind you all day of His faithfulness. Be open today to see, hear, and sense Him sending sweet kisses to you throughout the day.

_____

_____

Maybe an encouraging word from a friend, someone buying your coffee, finding something that was lost, or something in nature that He knows means something to you. Document it here or in your journal!

_____

Notes

Notes

DAY 17

Hello There Courageous One!

What three things are you grateful for today?

_____

_____

_____

_____

Honoring God Speaking

Reflection: in what ways has Papa been speaking to you?

_____

_____

_____

_____

_____

_____

_____

_____

*Scripture*

Psalm 16:5 TPT

"'Lord I have chosen you alone as my inheritance. You are my prize, my plea-sure, and my portion. I leave my destiny and its timing in your hands."

What stood out to you in this scripture?

_____

_____

_____

_____

The verse is laden with heartfelt cries of not only adoration but complete trust in the Father. David is not just saying he trusts the Lord with his heart and destiny, but that God is his everything, his future and the foundation of his future generations. I love this version because it declares prize, pleasure, and portion. He is not only the one who saves us, but gives us great pleasure loving Him back; and in that, He fills us up!

Activation

Let's practice exchanging our worries about things NOT happening in our lives (our destiny), for adoration of Him, just for 5 minutes. Put your timer on, and every thought of worry about your destiny, exchange it for a thought about His love. Think on who He is, how He fills you up. Write down the worry, then write on the opposite side but GOD IS...!

Notes

Notes

_____

_____

_____

_____

_____

_____

_____

_____

_____

_____

_____

_____

_____

_____

_____

_____

_____

_____

_____

_____

_____

DAY 18

Hello There Precious One!

What three things are you grateful for today?

_____

_____

_____

_____

Honoring God Speaking

Reflecting on yesterday, how did Papa speak to you?

_____

_____

_____

_____

_____

_____

_____

_____

Scripture

Psalms 18:30 TPT

"'What a God you are! Your path for me has been perfect! All your promises have proven true. What a secure shelter for all those who turn to hide them-selves in You! You are the wrap-around God giving grace to me."

Psalms 18:30 NKJV

"As for God, His way is perfect; the word of the Lord is proven; He is a shield to all who trust in Him."

SO good! What did Holy Spirit highlight to you in these scriptures? Was there overlap in a theme?

_____

_____

_____

_____

Activation

Sit still and close your eyes. See God wrapping His arms around you and comforting you in whatever area you need peace. Now listen, what is He saying about this area? What are you sensing?

_____

_____

_____

Notes

_____

_____

_____

_____

_____

_____

_____

_____

_____

_____

_____

_____

_____

_____

_____

_____

_____

_____

_____

_____

_____

_____

_____

_____

_____

_____

_____

_____

_____

_____

_____

_____

_____

_____

_____

_____

_____

_____

_____

_____

_____

DAY 19

Hello There Righteous One!

What three things are you grateful for today?

_____

_____

_____

_____

Honoring God Speaking

Reflecting on yesterday, how did Papa speak to you?

_____

_____

_____

_____

_____

_____

_____

_____

Scripture

1 Peter 5:6-7 TPT

"If you bow low in God's awesome presence, He will eventually exalt you as you leave the timing in His hands. Pour out all your worries and stress upon Him and leave them there, for He always tenderly cares for you."

So rich! Underline, then write here the part of the scripture that spoke to you most. Why do you think that is?

_____

_____

_____

_____

What stood out to me was, leaving the timing in His hands. It seems easy to trust Him orchestrating things, but I often get anxious about the timing. One of the beauties of the Lord is that He is outside of time; therefore, He has a perspective that is free from the constraints of time. But when we operate in fear or worry, we limit Him from revealing that perspective to us. This scripture reassures us that He tenderly cares for us! We can totally trust Him, that He is working all things for our good, AND in the perfect timing!

Activation

Write down three worries and ask the Lord what He says about them. Listen for a scripture, be sensitive to impressions; what pictures are you seeing in your mind? If you don't sense anything immediately, expect He will reveal something(s) throughout the day. Remember, BE AWARE. He wants to speak to us every day!!!

_____

_____

_____

Notes

DAY 20

Hello There Glorious One!

What three things are you grateful for today?

_____

_____

_____

_____

Honoring God Speaking

Reflecting on yesterday, how did you hear, sense, or see Papa speaking to you?

_____

_____

_____

_____

_____

_____

_____

_____

Titus 3:7-8 TPT

"'So as a gift of His love, and since we are faultless-innocent before His face- we can now become heirs of all things, all because of an overflowing hope of eternal life. How true and faithful is the message."

What jumped out at you from this scripture?

_____

_____

_____

_____

My heart leapt when I read that He not only makes us innocent, He makes us heirs of ALL things! We don't have shame, we have dignity! He considers us INNOCENT so we can be worthy to be heirs, to carry His favor, and to impact the sphere around us. This is powerful!!

Take 5 minutes to meditate on the words that stood out to you. Now reflect on how He has used various things already to speak hope to you. For example: Scripture, pictures, words spoken over you, songs, dreams, animals etc.)

Notes

Notes

_____

_____

_____

_____

_____

_____

_____

_____

_____

_____

_____

_____

_____

_____

_____

_____

_____

_____

_____

_____

DAY 21

Hello There Royal One!

What three things are you grateful for today?

_____

_____

_____

_____

Honoring God Speaking

Reflecting on yesterday. how did Papa speak to you?

_____

_____

_____

_____

_____

_____

_____

 *Scripture*

Hebrews 6:18 TPT

"'And now we have run into His heart to hide ourselves in His faithfulness. This is where we find His strength and comfort, for He empowers us to seize what has already been established ahead of time— an unshakeable hope!"

So rich! So what landed from that scripture?

_____

_____

_____

_____

For me this entire verse is so encouraging! I feel the steadfastness of the character of God when I read it. I know that as I hide myself in Him, the fullness of who He is, will manifest in my world. His unchanging character is my ROCK! His steadfast word is my anchor. His faithfulness knows no time limits, and His promises are outside of time. I can pull on them at any moment!

Activation

Put on some instrumental praise and meditate on this word. Read it aloud, two times. What keeps jumping out to you as you read it?
Write down those words. Ask God specifically where He sees you applying those words to your current situations or everyday life.

_____

_____

_____

_____

_____

Notes

Notes

DAY 22

Hello There Radiant One!

What three things are you grateful for today?

_____

_____

_____

_____

Honoring God Speaking

Reflecting on yesterday, how was Papa speaking to you?

_____

_____

_____

_____

_____

_____

_____

> # Isaiah 55:10–11 NKJV
>
> *"For as the rain comes down, and the snow from heaven, and do not return there, but it water the earth, and make it bring forth and bud, that it may give seed to the sower and bread to, the eater so shall My word be that goes forth from My mouth; it shall not return to Me void, but it shall accomplish what I please, and it shall prosper in the thing for which I sent it."*

So powerful, what did Holy Spirit highlight to you?

_____

_____

_____

_____

What I love about this scripture is the certainty it brings my heart. Knowing that I can pray the scripture back to the Lord, and that the full measure of the word that was spoken will be accomplished, is so anchoring to my soul!
I often pray the Apostolic prayers (ex: prayers in Colossians, Ephesians, and Philippians) I can feel the power of the words landing as I pray them over myself, and others.

Activation

Today meditate on how He has fulfilled His word in your life. Write down 5 ways you have seen His word manifest in your life. Some examples may include:

- Was He faithful to provide as He said He would be in Matthew 6?

- Did you feel His peace like Jesus refers to in John 16?

- Has your hope been restored as in Romans 12?

_____

_____

_____

_____

_____

95

Notes

Notes

DAY 23

Hello There Amazing One!

What three things are you grateful for today?

_____

_____

_____

_____

Honoring God Speaking

Reflecting on yesterday. how did you hear Papa speaking to you?

_____

_____

_____

_____

_____

_____

_____

_____

Scripture

Colossians 1:10-11 Amplified Version

" *so that you will walk in a manner worthy of the Lord (displaying admirable character, moral courage, and personal integrity) to (fully) please Him in all things, bearing fruit in every good work and steadily growing in the knowledge of God (with deeper faith, clearer insight and fervent love for His precepts) (we pray that you be) strengthened and invigorated with all power, according to His glorious might, to attain every kind of endurance and patience with joy, giving thanks to the Father, who has qualified us to share in the inheritance of the saints (God's people) in the Light.*"

So much here, what landed?

_____

_____

_____

_____

The encouragement this scripture brings to me is that Paul prays my heart. He gives me permission to go to the deepest places of insight into the Lord, to not only know His love, but to also be strengthened with power by it! Who doesn't want to be invigorated by God's beauty and strength?
I pray this apostolic prayer over those I care for, as well as myself, often. It tethers my heart to His heart for us all; and I trust His word will not return void!

Activation

Pray this prayer over yourself using the New King James version.
Now ask Holy Spirit for a name that you could use in this prayer as well.
Document whom you prayed for, and the date you prayed this over them.

Notes

Notes

DAY 24

Hello There Magnificent One!

What three things are you grateful for today?

_____

_____

_____

_____

Honoring God Speaking

Reflecting on yesterday. how did Papa speak to you?

_____

_____

_____

_____

_____

_____

_____

Scripture

1 Corinthians 2:9-10 TPT

"This is why the scriptures say: Things never discovered or heard of before, things beyond our ability to imagine—these are the many things God has in store for all His lovers. But God now unveils these profound realities to us by the Spirit. Yes, He has revealed to us His inmost heart and deepest mysteries through the Holy Spirit, who constantly explores all things."

Wow, so good! What jumped off the page when you read that scripture?

_____

_____

_____

_____

This scripture give me a sense of awe of the Lord. It reveals His heart TO me, and His heart FOR me. He wants us to know Him more deeply, but also wants us to have a joy as we discover more of the mysteries He wants to show us. The mysteries of how a wonderful God gives us the power to bring His Kingdom to the earth, and to live in power through His Holy Spirit!

Activation

Ask God what one mysterious facet of Himself He would like to reveal to you today.

Be alert as you go through your day listening, and being sensitive to what He may be using around you to speak to you. You may hear something in your prayer time. Then this week, look for that facet of Him all around you. Journal what you see, hear, sense, or just have a knowing about.

Notes

Notes

DAY 25

Hello Hopeful One!

What three things are you grateful for today?

_____

_____

_____

_____

Honoring God Speaking

Reflecting on yesterday. how did hear or sense Papa speaking to you?

_____

_____

_____

_____

_____

_____

_____

_____

Scripture

Philippians 4:8 The Passion Translation

"So keep your thoughts continually fixed on all that is authentic and real, honorable and admirable, beautiful and respectful, pure and holy, merciful and kind. And fasten your thoughts on every glorious work of God, praising Him always."

One of my favorites! What is highlighted as you read this scripture?

_____

_____

_____

_____

This devotional journal has a two-fold purpose; to honor how God is speaking to us in both word, and by His Spirit in our everyday lives. It is super important that as we journey, we keep our thoughts toward Him, and the beauty He offers us each, and every day. As we are diligent to do as this scripture says, to think upon the most brilliant things, we are fulfilling instruction of renewing our minds, and being transformed by it.

Proverbs 23:7 says "As a man thinketh in his heart, so is he." KJV
In other words, you will manifest in your behavior what you have been thinking about. This reiterates our need to focus on the wonderful things God has done for us, and the beauty of His character, so that we too will manifest His beauty in our lives!

Activation

Write down ten beautiful things in your life: Is it your family? God's faithfulness? Your friends?

Now today, when a negative thought comes, flip it into a positive, and think about either something you wrote down, or something beautiful you may have seen throughout the day- like an act of kindness you saw someone show, or a lovely sunset.

_____

_____

_____

_____

_____

_____

_____

_____

_____

_____

_____

_____

_____

_____

_____

_____

_____

_____

_____

_____

_____

Notes

DAY 26

Hello Faithful One!

What three things are you grateful for today?

_____

_____

_____

_____

Honoring God Speaking

Reflecting on yesterday. how did Papa speak to you?

_____

_____

_____

_____

_____

_____

_____

> ## Daniel 2:22 NKJV
> *"It is He who reveals the profound and hidden things; He knows what is in the darkness, and the light dwells with him."*

What are you attracted to most about this scripture? Why?

_____

_____

_____

_____

For me, this scripture is an actual testimony of God speaking to me through numbers and patterns. I often wake up at this exact time 2:22, or see this number sequence, several days in a row. After taking note of the time, I ask Holy Spirit what book of the bible it is.

I once sensed Acts so I looked it up. This verse speaks of signs, wonders, and miracles. I liked that, and felt encouraged that Holy Spirit was affirming me in walking in the miraculous. Then it came time to prepare for this day, and I sensed Holy Spirit encouraging me to look at Daniel 2:22.

Firstly, I had already underlined that scripture at some point. Secondly, I thought, how appropriate since that is what this devotional is all about- revealing His heart for us in the secret things!

It is His good pleasure to do so, and in this regard, many things were accomplished by Daniel interpreting Nebuchadnezzar's dream. How do we know that we are sensing or seeing won't be influential to the lives around us?! God is both multifaceted and multitasking, and He loves connection! This makes it more likely than not!

Ask Holy Spirit to show you some things He's been using over the last week to send you a message, one that will cause you to delve into the secret things God wants to reveal to you. What did He show you?

_____

Now, ask Him for a scripture. You may get a sense of the book, or number, or even just one that you have memorized pop in your head. Write it down!

Notes

Notes

DAY 27

Hello Glorious One!

What three things are you grateful for today?

_____

_____

_____

_____

Honoring God Speaking

Reflecting on yesterday. how did you hear Papa speaking to you?

_____

_____

_____

_____

_____

_____

_____

_____

Scripture

Colossians 3:1-2 MSG

"So if you are serious about living this new resurrection life with Christ, act like it. Pursue the things over which Christ presides. Don't shuffle along, eyes to the ground, absorbed with the things right in front of you. Look up, and be alert to what is going on around Christ-that's where the action is. See things from His perspective."

Not a light scripture, but rich! What hit home in your heart?

_____

_____

_____

_____

It is so easy to get caught up in the distractions of life, and grow dull to the things of the Spirit. We can also become so principle driven that we forget to honor the relationship part that requires intentionality, and awareness, to the nuances of God speaking to us.
I love how Paul says, "Look up!" I practice this when I am getting consumed, and feeling disconnected from Holy Spirit- I look up, casting my eyes on the prize of Christ Jesus!

Activation

Put on your favorite worship song. Now close your eyes, and listen to the words. What pictures are elicited from the song? What feelings?

_____

_____

_____

So what facet of God do you connect with most through this song? Is it His Father's heart? His faithfulness? His lovingkindness?

_____

_____

Notes

Notes

DAY 28

Hello Powerful One!

What three things are you grateful for today?

_____

_____

_____

_____

Honoring God Speaking

Reflecting on yesterday, how did Papa speak to you?

_____

_____

_____

_____

_____

_____

_____

Scripture

> ## Psalms 118:27-29 TPT
> *"For the Lord our God has brought us His glory-light. I offer Him my life in joyous sacrifice. Tied tightly to your altar I will bring you praise. For you are the God of my life and I lift you high, exalting you to the highest place. So let's keep on giving our thanks to God, for He is so good! His constant, tender love lasts forever!"*

What did Holy Spirit highlight to you in this verse?

_____

_____

_____

_____

Light makes me smile! I am a sunshine girl, so any verse associated with the Light of God makes my heart sing!

Often we get caught up in the knowing about God, and forget the beauty of just who He is...the awe of His majestic essence. Basking in that understanding is a win-win. We relish in His beauty, worship Him, and simultaneously, are filled with wonder and joy!

His constant, tender love lasts FOREVER!

Activation

Meditate on the beauty of the Lord. In the book of Revelation, John discusses the throne of the Lord. How majestic that vision must have been! Throughout the day, make note of where you see the beauty of the Lord in Creation!

_____

_____

_____

Notes

_____

_____

_____

_____

_____

_____

_____

_____

_____

_____

_____

_____

_____

_____

_____

_____

_____

_____

_____

Notes

_____

_____

_____

_____

_____

_____

_____

_____

_____

_____

_____

_____

_____

_____

_____

_____

_____

_____

_____

_____

_____

_____

DAY 29

Hello Amazing One!

What three things are you grateful for today?

_____

_____

_____

_____

Honoring God Speaking

Reflecting on yesterday. how did hear/ sense Papa speaking to you?

_____

_____

_____

_____

_____

_____

_____

_____

> ## Psalms 119:15-16 NKJV
> *"'I will meditate on Your precepts, and contemplate Your ways. I will delight myself in Your statutes. I will not forget your word."*

What is speaking to you most in this scripture? What do you hear Holy Spirit speaking to your heart through it?

_____

_____

_____

_____

The word statutes in the Merriam Webster dictionary, means: a written law created by government, a written rule or regulation.
To delight in God's precepts which are also statutes, is to be joyful to walk in them, to not forget His word.
Sometimes we equate this with rules of behavior rather than Rev. 19:13 which says, Jesus was the word- His name is called the Word of God.
As Bill Johnson says, "Jesus is perfect theology." So when I think about meditating on statutes, I think about meditating on what Jesus said, and lived. These are the precepts of God, these are the written laws of the Kingdom-His very life!
He said love God, and love your neighbor, that these are the greatest precepts. When I meditate on what He says is the greatest, my behavior lines up with what I am meditating on. This is what causes this scripture to come to life for me. Jesus relentless pursuit of us has assured us that what He says, can be counted on! His life, death, and resurrection are proof of the loving character of our God!

Activation

What are the words Jesus spoke that really resonate with you in this season? Write it down to remind yourself now so that you can reflect and meditate on those as well as scriptures. Look for the evidence of those things manifesting in your life!

_____

_____

Notes

Notes

DAY 30

Hello Victorious One!

What three things are you grateful for today?

_____

_____

_____

_____

Honoring God Speaking

Reflecting on yesterday. what are some ways you heard Papa speak to you?

_____

_____

_____

_____

_____

_____

_____

Psalms 95:7-8

"For He is our God and we are the people of His pasture and the sheep of His hand. Today, if you will hear His voice, do not harden your hearts and become spiritually dull as at Meribah {the place of strife}, and as at Massah {the place of testing} in the wilderness..."

What is landing in your heart and spirit when you read this scripture?

_____

_____

_____

_____

This entire devotional is about hearing God and trusting in Him. Trusting that He is the anchor of our hope. As we reflect on this reminder to stay alert, we have to protect against the activities of this life dulling our hearts and minds. It is easy to grow hard to the still, small voice Holy Spirit is speaking through each and everyday, if we get consumed with the mundane of life. We want to stay alert to the patterns, signs, words, and kisses that He sends us throughout the day!

Activation

Make a list of 10 ways you have heard God speaking to you over the last 30 days, whether through seeing, hearing, sensing, or just a deep sense of knowing.

_____

_____

_____

_____

_____

_____

_____

Notes

Notes

Made in the USA
Lexington, KY
27 August 2019